THIS BOOK is to
commemorate the issuance of the
official Three Affiliated Tribes medal
February 1, 1974
and is limited to 15,000 copies
No. **LIBRARY**

Malnamie

Painting by Karl Bodmer, Courtesy University of South Dakota Library

AS THE THREE AFFILIATED TRIBES integrate into the modern industrial economy and grow in population, it is well to remember that they survived many grim periods during the 19th Century, as symbolized in this painting of "Mandan Idols."

THE
THREE
AFFILIATED
TRIBES
(MANDAN, ARIKARA, AND HIDATSA)

by Joseph H. Cash
and Gerald W. Wolff

Scientific Editor: Henry F. Dobyns
General Editor: John I. Griffin

PUBLISHED BY INDIAN TRIBAL SERIES / PHOENIX

Library of Congress Catalog Number 74-75453

PRINTED IN THE UNITED STATES OF AMERICA — Imperial Lithographers

THREE AFFILIATED TRIBES CHAIRMAN VINCENT MALNOURIE

VINCENT MALNOURIE was born on March 21, 1910, to Charles and Daisy Little Sioux Duckett Malnourie in the Beaver Creek District of Fort Berthold Indian Reservation. That District lies south of the fortified Earth Lodge Village ("Like-A-Fish-Hook") and was occupied by the Arikara, Mandan and Hidatsa tribes known as the "Three Affiliated Tribes."

Young Malnourie attended the Pierre Indian School in Pierre, South Dakota, and then Sherman Institute in Riverside, California. After graduating from the latter institution in 1932, he became an employee of the United States Bureau of Indian Affairs in 1937.

World War II interrupted, and Vincent Malnourie joined the United States Navy. Returning home, Malnourie continued his employment in the Bureau of Indian Affairs for a total of thirty years.

Upon his retirement in 1968, Malnourie was elected to the Tribal Business Council on the Fort Berthold Reservation. In 1968, he was elected Tribal Chairman. Reelected in 1970, he is currently serving out his second term.

As a councilman and particularly as Tribal Chairman, Vincent Malnourie can point with pride to the growth and accomplishment that is under way throughout the Fort Berthold Reservation.

MATÓ-TOPE A MANDAN CHIEF

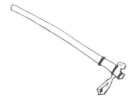

HIGH ON THE MISSOURI, above the White, the Cheyenne, and the Cannonball Rivers, is the Fort Berthold Reservation. Here dwell the remnants of three famed Indian nations — once great, later decimated, and now reviving in a struggle to regain their former glories. They are the Mandan, the Arikara, and the Hidatsa. Together they form the Three Affiliated Tribes.

Their story is one of courage in the face of adversity and recurring disaster. Their greatest attribute is the ability to survive and persist. Living in an inhospitable region, surrounded by enemies, and faced with decisions concerning events over which they have little control, they have held together and now approach a newer and better world. Through all of this they have maintained their original identities while gathering strength from their unity. They are similar, yet different. They insist on retaining their identity and being what they are in the new world that they are rapidly mastering.

1

Few American Indian people have fascinated the white men as have the Mandan. Few have had more significance than the Mandan. Early travelers to the reaches of the Upper Missouri admired these people and were intrigued by what they considered to be their light coloring and the presence of blue eyes. They immediately concluded that these were not really American Indians but the descendants of Europeans who at one time or another had come to the New World, had stayed, and ultimately had forgotten their European origins. There was one theory that the Mandans were part of the ten lost tribes of Israel, and yet another that claimed they were the descendants of Irish monks. In particular, George Catlin advanced the notion that they were descendants of the Welsh, and the famed artist spent much of his life trying to trace similarities between the Mandan and Welsh languages. He was convinced that his idea was correct. Fortunately, he proved to be a better painter than linguist. The Mandans are American Indians and deserve attention because of who they were and what they did.

While the speculations about the European origins of the Mandans are discounted today, there is another theory that has been widely published and accepted. It states that the Mandans no longer exist and are, in fact, extinct.

This theory is well known among the Mandans themselves, and they react to it with amusement, scorn, and on occasion, outrage. Surely the ultimate insult a man can receive is to be told that he is extinct. This schema is based on certain premises, the predominant one being that there are no longer any fullblood Mandan Indians, which may be true. It also finds roots in the fact that Mandan culture has undergone considerable change over the years and is no longer in its pure state. Yet it is hard to argue against the strong feeling that the Mandans do indeed exist as long as there are people who speak the Mandan language and who proudly proclaim themselves to be Mandan. They not only exist, but they live in pride and accomplishment.

The origins of the Mandans, like those of most Native American peoples, have their details hidden in the shrouds of time. It is almost certain that they existed in the Ohio River Valley, and it is possible that prior to that they were located in the southeastern United States. Linguistically, they are part of the great Siouan family of languages, and like the Plains Sioux, they apparently moved from the Ohio River country to the north and west, eventually striking the Missouri River – perhaps in South Dakota – and later moving up-river into what is now North Dakota. It now seems apparent that the first Mandan penetration to the Missouri

3

River took place as early as 1250 A.D. Some went into southern Minnesota, some into northeastern Iowa. One group evidently entered South Dakota and went up the Missouri, while another group went directly from Minnesota into North Dakota. It has been suggested that in this early period of movement the Mandans were divided into a northern branch that centered in North Dakota and northern South Dakota, and a southern branch that was located in southeastern South Dakota. The evidence is not entirely clear. During this period, the Mandans apparently lived in small villages, with an average population of about 200 people each, without a very complex form of centralized government, and with distinct differences in the cultures of the sundry villages. These villages were typically located on high ground overlooking the bottomland of rivers. This allowed them to put together a village that could be defended, to build their semi-sunken earthlodges, and to construct fortifications. It is quite certain that these people had an economy that was based on both hunting and agriculture. They would hunt buffalo, as well as smaller game, on foot. On their small farms in the bottomlands, the Mandans produced mainly corn, beans, and squash. They were a people who consistently planned ahead and who stored their agricultural products to sustain them during bad years.

By 1600, the Mandans were fortifying their villages by building stockades around them; in many cases, they built villages on the bluffs above the river so that only one side had to be palisaded. By this time, they also were attacked by some foe, apparently a group of nomadic Indians. In this period, the horse had not yet been introduced to the Northern Plains, and so they came on foot. As a counter to this handicap in mobility, the Mandans began to concentrate. Smaller villages combined, until there were seven large ones – three on the east bank of the Missouri and four on the west side. At this same time, they also began to build their distinctive large round lodges that were approximately forty feet in diameter. By doing this, they were able to crowd more people into less space. It was also during this time that they ceased putting their lodges in rows with streets separating them, but rather crowded them together.

By 1700, the Mandans had developed many of the basic characteristics of their civilization. They had borrowed certain things from other people. From the eastern woodland area, they had adopted pottery-making and some ceremonies. From the so-called Plains culture came their great ceremony, the Okeepa, and buffalo hunting. By then, approximately six to eight thousand Mandans were living near the mouth of the Heart River; that area represented one of the major concentrations of population in the Northern Plains. Other people also borrowed from them, and it is very likely that the feathered headdress of the Plains Indians — that which the Sioux call the Wapaha — was a Mandan creation. They were also a trading people who exchanged their corn for hides and other goods obtained from the Cheyenne, who came to them on horseback at this time from western South Dakota near the Black Hills. It was also during this time span that the Mandan first began to receive white trade goods from the Assiniboines, who in turn had gotten them from the Englishmen to the east.

The Mandans at the turn of the eighteenth century were on the verge of great changes — some happy, more not. They were a strong people who knew how to live in the cold of Plains winters and to survive the heat and drought of the summers. They had developed a knack for group living, for trade, and for manufacture. At this point, one might reasonably expect their culture to rise to higher and higher levels of sophistication, and for their history to become more glorious; but other events beyond their control intervened.

THE MANDAN OKEEPA CEREMONY

Nearly every tribe that inhabited the Great Plains sooner or later adopted the sun dance

Painting by Karl Bodmer, Courtesy University of South Dakota Library
MANDANS EMPLOYED MARKEDLY DIFFERENT TECHNOLOGIES during the cold winters and hot summers on the Northern Great Plains. During the winter, they trans-
ported people and possessions on toboggans pulled by working dogs, selectively bred
and specially trained. During the summer, these dogs hauled pole travois.

ceremony, wherein fasting, prayers, and some-times self-torture occurred before the final climactic act. In this act, the dancers' chests were pierced, and a skewer was placed through the chest muscles and attached by a rawhide rope to a central pole. The dancers pulled against the rope while dancing, all the while facing the sun. They attempted to tear loose the skewers that pierced their flesh, and while most succeeded, some still hung attached when the sun went down. This ceremony had different nuances and variations from tribe to tribe.

The Mandans performed a ceremony that was different from the sun dance, although there were similarities. It has been speculated that perhaps the sun dance had its origins in the Mandan Okeepa. The Okeepa ceremony basically involved a retelling of events from the distant past. It did not take place in the open around a pole as in the case of the sun dance, but rather in the Okeepa lodge, which was very large and built of logs. The ceremony was offered in fulfillment of a vow based on a dream, and the participants were chosen accord-ing to clan membership and bundle rights. The major practical result, and all Plains religious ceremonies were supposed to lead to practical results, was to ensure the prosperity of the people, and particularly to bring the buffalo.

During the ceremony, the participants beat on drums, rattled percussion instruments, and imper-

THE BUFFALO DANCE of the Mandan tribe as painted by Karl Bodmer.

sonated mythical and animal characters. Part of the ceremony, which lasted for days, included the bull dance, where the dancers painted themselves, wore masks made from the skin of buffalo heads, and carried bundles of willow twigs on their backs. On the last day, the dancers were pierced as in the sun dance — skewers thrust through their chest muscles and tied to ropes — whereupon they were hoisted above the ground and hung suspended in the air until they tore loose. Some of them would also pierce their backs and hang the heads, skills, or hides of buffalo from them. The pain was intense. Other men would dance and move around the village, dragging objects attached to their piercings.

When the Bureau of Indian Affairs secured control of the reservations and brought in the missionaries, these ceremonies were in effect outlawed on the grounds that they were barbarous. From a present-day perspective, however, one can only think that Christianity at the height of its fervor also practiced debasement of the flesh for a greater end, and that religious ecstasy coming out of physical pain is found in many societies the world over. The physical manifestations of the Indian religion, such as those seen in the sun dance and Okeepa, seem to be part of an ancient tradition, if not an innate urge, among human beings to commit themselves to high and noble beliefs and, on occasion, to suffer severely for those beliefs.

10

The origins of the Arikara are, if anything, more obscure than those of the Mandans. In some ways, they are the most unique of the Three Affiliated Tribes. Their language, unlike the Mandan and Hidatsa, does not come from the Siouan group, but rather stems from the Caddoan. The Arikara are the northernmost people of this linguistic group, and are separated by distance and by culture from their kin. Their name, the Arikara, was corrupted into the term "Ree" by the early explorers and fur traders, and one finds this name in many early accounts and on features of the land area of the Northern Plains. Before the Arikara moved north, they were given their name by their fellows, the Skidi Pawnee, and it meant "horns." Apparently this came from their custom of wearing pieces of bone in their hair.

It is not known for certain why the Arikara came north. They had been living along the Loup River in Nebraska with their relatives. Yet sometime during the seventeenth century, they separated and moved or were driven northward. They do not regard themselves as the offshoot of the Pawnee, but rather quite the reverse. They argue that the Pawnee are an offshoot of the Arikara who lacked the necessary spirit to change locales. In any case, perhaps driven by drought, perhaps pushed by the Sioux people, they moved up the great highway of the west — the Missouri River. They settled in various village sites in South Dakota along the Missouri, after having entered the area near the eastern edge of what is now Gregory County. Some massive remains of what are assumed to be Arikara villages have been found near Pierre and near Fort Thompson. One of these discoveries indicates that the Arikara had dug moats and thrown up battlements in order to use crossfire on their approaching enemies. This device had previously been regarded as an exclusively European invention. The Arikara continued their trek up the river, always building fortified sites on the bluffs. Apparently, they had at one time lived as far south as Omaha. Later, they migrated and joined the Mandans, quarreled with them, and moved south again. In 1770, French traders found them on the Missouri below the Cheyenne River. By 1804, they were in North Dakota in three large villages between the Grand and Cannonball Rivers.

Arikara culture was not terribly different from that of the Mandans. They made pottery by the coil method. They also cultivated corn, beans, and squash; and corn became so prominent in their diet and their trade that in Indian sign language they became known as the "corn-eaters." The Arikara were especially noteworthy for their development of trade with other Indians. Corn and other dried foods were

HE FAMOUS MANDAN VILLAGE on a bluff overlooking the Missouri River, with omen crossing that stream in buffalo-hide "bull-boats."

swapped for hides and meat from the more nomadic Indians. The Arikara were especially adept at decorating hides and became famed throughout the whole region for their work. Thus, they would trade for the raw hides and convert them into the finished product, which would then be sold for the wherewithal to buy still more hides. The Arikara were probably the first of the tribes on the Upper Missouri to acquire the horse, obtaining it in 1738. Great traders that they were, they successfully turned the horse to commercial use, acquiring their stock from the south and trading it to the tribes in their own area — thus again serving as middlemen. The horse trade was very useful and very lucrative, but had within it the seeds of Arikara destruction. In this early period, the Arikara were the major suppliers of horses to the Sioux who had originally come to them on foot, grateful for any favors. When the Sioux received horses in sufficient numbers, they became the brilliant plumed warriors of fact and fable, turning on their former benefactors. Under these conditions, the Sioux provided the pressure of arms that inevitably forced the Arikara into wars and just as inevitably pressured them into retreating farther and farther up the river.

THE SACRED BUNDLES

Most of the tribes that resided on the Great Plains had some form of sacred medicine bundle.

14

The word "medicine" had special connotations and, in essence, meant that it provided a special contact with the supernatural. Some bundles were individually owned, while others were the property of bands, societies, clans, and even tribes.

The Arikara had ten tribal bundles provided by the Corn Mother. One belonged to each of the ten bands of the tribe. These bundles were opened in the spring and were used in a reenactment of the tribe's origin, and also to ensure good crops. Contained in these bundles were ears of corn, knives, animal skins, bird skins, and other objects. Attached to them on the outside were five large gourd rattles.

The Mandans and Hidatsa also had bundles, but each was owned by a small group within a clan and could be inherited or transferred. When the ownership of a bundle was transferred, a feast was given and elaborate ceremonies were conducted. Among the Mandan, individuals also possessed bundles, constructed from information gleaned from their own personal visions, and these bundles could be transferred to other individuals. Their importance was not so much tribal as individual; and it was believed that they could give strength and support to the warriors who owned them.

Perhaps the most unusual medicine bundle of all was the Big Bird's bundle, which was owned by the Midipati clan of the Hidatsa. This clan was known as the "water-buster" clan, and its bundle became known in turn as the "water-buster" bundle. This bundle was used to bring rain and allegedly was very effective. Its history took an interesting turn in the 1930's. This bundle had come into the possession of a New York collector shortly after the turn of the century. During the 1930's, when the long and terrible droughts hit the plains, the tribe requested that it be returned, and it was brought back to the reservation. It is said that after the first "water-buster" ceremony, North Dakota was blessed with an extensive and much welcomed rainfall.

HIDATSA ORIGINS

The largest of the Three Affiliated Tribes is the Hidatsa, and it is also the least known and most difficult of the trio to trace. Part of the reason for this difficulty lies in the fact that throughout recorded history the Hidatsa have been known by so many different names. The most common of these is the Gros Ventres, which translates as "Big Bellies." This term was assigned to them by Frenchmen who mistook them for the Atsina, who are also known as Gros Ventres. The third name, which appears frequently in the accounts of the early travelers along the Missouri, is Minitaree, which can be

BIG BIRD'S MEDICINE BUNDLE, property of the Hidatsa Midipati or "Water-buster" Clan. When the last Midipati custodian, Slim Shin, died prior to 1900, clansmen feared to replace him while federal officials suppressed native religion. His son, a Prairie Chicken clansman, sold it to a missionary in 1907; the latter resold it to a New York city museum. In 1938, tribal Chairman Arthur Mandan led negotiations to recover it with aid from a reformed Bureau of Indian Affairs.

spelled in several ways, and means the "People Across the Water." Apparently, it is a term applied to them by the Mandans. The Hidatsa — and this term may mean "People of the Willows" or may be the name of the village in antiquity on the Knife River — came from a common group of Siouan speaking peoples, which included the Crow. According to their own legends, the Hidatsa originated from people who climbed a grapevine under the earth and emerged from the waters of Devil's Lake in present-day North Dakota and later migrated westward. At this time, they were as one with the Crow. Then the tribe split in the late seventeenth century because of a disagreement between the wives of two chiefs over the contents of a buffalo stomach. After a brief battle, the group which would become known as the Crow moved to the west, and the Hidatsa remained essentially in what is now North Dakota. The Hidatsa eventually moved southwest and became the allies of the Mandans, who in all probability taught them to build the circular lodge and how to cultivate squash, corn, pumpkins, and beans. Through all of this, however, the Hidatsa continued to reflect the hunting traditions of the Plains Indians to a much greater extent than either the Mandans or the Arikara.

Sometime before the turn of the nineteenth century, the Mandans and the Hidatsa both made their way up the Missouri to the vicinity of the Knife River where they were residing when Lewis and Clark came upriver. It was a Hidatsa war party that captured the famed Shoshone girl, Sakakawea, from her people and traded her to the Frenchman, Charbonneau. Charbonneau, in turn, took Sakakawea and her infant son along with the Lewis and Clark expedition, where on several occasions she proved invaluable.

The Hidatsa were living in three villages near the mouth of the Knife River when Lewis and Clark visited them in 1804. They were still at the same point when Maximilian of Wied arrived in 1833. After the great smallpox epidemics of 1837, however, they formed a new village with the Mandans at Fish-hook Bend on the Missouri River. It was here that Fort Berthold was built, and it was here that the Arikara finally joined the other two in 1862.

Of the Three Affiliated Tribes, the Hidatsa were more nearly the nomadic Plains warriors through much of their existence. After they had settled in villages and learned agriculture and lodge building from the Mandans, they continued to hunt on the plains more than the other two tribes. They warred occasionally with other Indian tribes and had even fought the Arikara in an earlier day. Yet they never fought the white man, and they always retained cordial relations with the Crow.

The Mandan, Arikara, and Hidatsa were fundamentally agricultural Indians. They hunted to supplement their agriculture. Raising any kind of crop high on the Upper Missouri was a difficult process and required great skill on the part of the cultivators. The growing season was short, drought years frequent, and the work hard.

Over the centuries, these Indians developed ways of adapting to their environment. They developed new strains of crops that suited the area. Raising beans, sunflowers, squash, pumpkins, tobacco, and corn, in almost every case their crops had been bred by deliberate processes that are still marvels to botanists. For example, the Hidatsa had nine distinct varieties of corn, five varieties of beans, and several varieties of squash. None of the tribes cultivated trees, root crops, or perennials.

Their farming techniques required hand work with the simplest of tools. For several reasons, these three peoples had always done their farming on the river bottoms and not on the prairies. One was that the soil of the river bottoms tended to be richer, and the moisture more sure. The other prime reason was that the prairies and plains of the uplands were covered with tough buffalo grass which required immense labor to break and till. On the other

OWL WOMAN, A HIDATSA, hoeing a corn hill, following the aboriginal division of labor. Her hoe consists of a buffalo shoulder blade hafted to a wooden handle. Behind Owl Woman stand sunflower plants which luxuriated on the edges of corn fields. The three tribes harvested their oil-rich seeds.

hand, the forested river bottoms had softer soil and after the trees were removed, basically by burn and slash methods, easy to work. The women did most of the work, although sometimes the men too old to be hunters and warriors would help with planting and weaving, and men's societies would sometimes cooperate in the corn harvest. For the most part, however, the ladies did it all and used digging sticks and bone hoes with which to till the soil. The hoe was made by fastening a buffalo shoulder blade to a wooden handle. Rakes were made of deer antlers and sometimes of bent willows.

Corn was the basic crop and was planted by hand in hills. These hills were arranged in rows, with each mound approximately four feet from the other in order to compensate for the lack of moisture. In wetter regions, the hills would have been much closer together. The corn was planted late in May and the seeds pressed by hand into the worked ground. Later, when the plants were a few inches high, the ground around them was hoed; still later when the corn silk had appeared, it was again cultivated. At the time of the last cultivation, the earth was piled around the stalks to protect the roots and to prevent the stalks from being blown over by the high winds of the area.

The Indians did not use scarecrows to keep the birds and rodents away from their crops.

Rather, they built platforms where women and girls stayed and guarded the corn, singing and doing handiwork. Armed men would patrol the fields to protect the women.

The corn and other crops, when harvested, were either eaten immediately or dried and stored. Much of the corn was eaten in the roasting ear stage, and the remainder was dried and either shelled or braided into long strings. The best ears were saved for seed for the next year. Dried food was stored in cache pits dug between the lodges in the village and sometimes underneath the floors of the lodges themselves. Hidatsa caches were dug with small openings that widened so that a bell-shape was achieved. They were large enough that a ladder was needed to get to the bottom. These storage pits were floored with split logs, lined with grass, and, after being filled, roofed with split poles and covered with earth so that only the owners could locate them. Thus, an enemy might destroy a village and think that he had wiped out the food supply of the people. Yet they could come back later, dig up their secret pits, and still find stored food intact.

Much of the dried food was eaten as winter rations together with dried meat. The Hidatsa in particular prepared a dish called "four-vegetables-mixed" which was composed of corn, beans, dried squash, and sunflower seeds. They also made bread from green corn, and mush and various other dishes made from their produce. Although they did not have salt and pepper, they would sometimes use a salt taken from alkali springs.

The cultivated foods were supplemented by the use of wild plants; in particular, they cherished the tipsina plant, which is frequently called the Indian turnip. This root was dug with sticks, cleaned, braided into long strings, and dried. In this manner, they kept indefinitely. The tipsina was used especially for boiling with meat. Women also gathered great amounts of June berries, buffalo berries, and choke-cherries for food. These were beaten with a stone hammer, patted into cakes, and dried in the sun. They could then be eaten as they were, boiled, or mixed with corn and tallow into corn balls. They could also be mixed with pounded dried meat and animal fat into the dish known most commonly as pemmican. Some of the Mandan, Arikara, and Hidatsa made sugar. They learned this from the Dakota and Chippewa, who had made sugar from maple trees in their original dwelling areas in Minnesota. When these two groups moved onto the plains, they discovered that the only species of maple was the box elder tree. They made a kind of maple sugar from these trees and the Three Affiliated Tribes followed their example.

In addition to the dietary functions of the many wild plants, there were, of course, medicinal and ceremonial functions. The medicine men had a wider choice of pharmaceuticals than did white doctors in the early eighteenth century, and numbers of them have been adopted by modern medicine. In ceremonies, some plants were used as a sort of incense by placing them on live coals to produce an aromatic smoke. Among these are sweetgrass, sage, and cedar.

All in all, the three tribes had developed a remarkably variant type of agriculture that showed skill and knowledge. They especially should be complimented for adapting to a region that was not noticeably hospitable to farmers and making a success of it. Their ability to adapt allowed for the stability of their society and let them develop settled villages. They did not drift into total nomadism. The Hidatsa, who had been nomadic, preferred the settled life when they joined the Mandans — thus, agriculture was the great settler.

HUNTING

Although the Mandans, Arikara, and Hidatsa practiced intensive agriculture, they supplemented it by hunting. As they had no domesticated animals, except for the dog, prior to the introduction of the horse from white sources, it was necessary that they hunt if they wanted to eat meat. The most important of the animals hunted was the buffalo. Indeed, it was so significant that the major ceremony of each tribe was centered about this great animal.

Hunting buffalo without a horse or a high-powered rifle is a difficult thing, and the people on the High Plains developed techniques that allowed it to be done successfully. The best method was by using the "buffalo jump." The hunters drove small herds of buffalo over a cliff or a cutbank so that the fall would kill or disable most of the animals. The other way was to attempt to sneak into a herd and attack a buffalo, man against beast. This was sometimes a losing proposition. On other occasions, an old bull or crippled animal might be picked off by a hunter or group of hunters on foot.

The coming of the horse revolutionized this style of hunting. Men on horseback could surround a herd and pursue the animals, shooting as many as possible with arrows. There are recorded instances of mounted warriors driving hunting arrows completely through the body of the buffaloes. They would also occasionally ride into a herd disguised, with buffalo robes thrown over them and their horses, and then suddenly start launching arrows at the unsuspecting bison.

Every part of the buffalo was used. The internal organs were frequently eaten raw. The

26

Courtesy Paul A. Ewald

RED CALF WOMAN stirring the contents of a cooking pot suspended from a tripod over her Mandan-style small-blaze fire. Meat dries in the sun on her drying pole. Red Calf Woman's son Arthur Mandan later served as interpreter, and tribal Chairman soon after the reservation residents adopted representative government in 1936.

flesh was cooked fresh or jerked and dried for later use; some of it would be made into pemmican. The hides were tanned to make robes, lodge covers, clothing, and bags. The large sinews were dried and split to use as thread. Spoons were made from the horns. Shoulder blades were made into hoes. The tool for fleshing skins was made from buffalo bones. The paunch was dried and used as a water container. Bullboats were made from the whole skins tied on a willow frame. There are few instances of any animal being so completely used.

In addition to the buffalo, they also hunted elk, antelope, and deer. Mountain sheep were especially prized, and from these animals the finer hides were used for making clothing. Porcupines were killed in order to obtain the quills, which were used for decoration. When the fur trade came, beaver, mink, fox, wildcat, martin, ermine, otter, and muskrat were trapped for their trade value.

The Mandans, Arikara, and Hidatsa, like their enemies the Cheyenne and Lakota, also caught eagles. A dedicated warrior dug a pit at the top of a hill and covered it with a lattice of poles, leaves, and other camouflage. A dead rabbit might be put on top of this to bait the eagle, while the Indian brave huddled underneath. When the eagle landed, the warrior grabbed him by his legs and killed him by strangulation. One may be sure that the eagles got their licks in before their demise. All of the procedures used for trapping eagles, which were sacred, were accompanied by ceremonies of the highest order. The feathers of the eagle were of great importance, and used in the headdresses and in various ceremonies that symbolized the many exploits in war. As an example of how closely these people were tied to nature, the Hidatsa claimed that their eagle trapping rites were given them originally by black bears.

THE FUR TRADE AND ITS EFFECTS

The major device by which white civilization made contact with the Indians and commenced the long process of altering their civilization was the fur trade. For two centuries this trade was the principal business on the frontier, and one practiced by all the nations in North America. The French pioneered this American fur trade. Joliet, LaSalle, Verendrye, among others, were sent to explore, largely because the French government wanted to establish a fur trade. The British quickly got into the act, and the Company of Gentlemen Adventurers of Hudson Bay became the greatest of all the fur trading companies, and one that penetrated into the regions inhabited by the Mandans, Arikara, and Hidatsa. Even this great company was not without competition, as the British North West

29

Company began in the late 1780's and prospered and struggled against the Hudson Bay enterprise. The Indians, of course, were caught in the middle of this rivalry, and at times they were able to play off one company against the other to their own advantage. Usually, however, they would up the victims of a tug-of-war, which they never completely understood, as they were buffeted and assailed from both sides. By 1811, the Hudson Bay and North West Companies were struggling over broad areas, mainly to the northwest of Lake Superior. The southern boundaries of these lands were the Mandan villages on the Missouri, close to the present-day town of Bismark. In this battle for supremacy, Hudson Bay established the Earl of Selkirk in the Red River Valley near the present city of Winnipeg and he, in turn, cut the lines of the North West Company. There was actual warfare, and lives were lost. Indians were dragged into the fray as participants, and as a result, the fur trade suffered. Ultimately, Hudson Bay won the contest and absorbed its rivals in 1821. This did not end the trouble, however, because new rivals were already coming on the scene from the young and expanding nation to the southeast, the United States.

In the early years of the nineteenth century, the Louisiana Purchase included the Upper Missouri region, and the Lewis and Clark expedi-

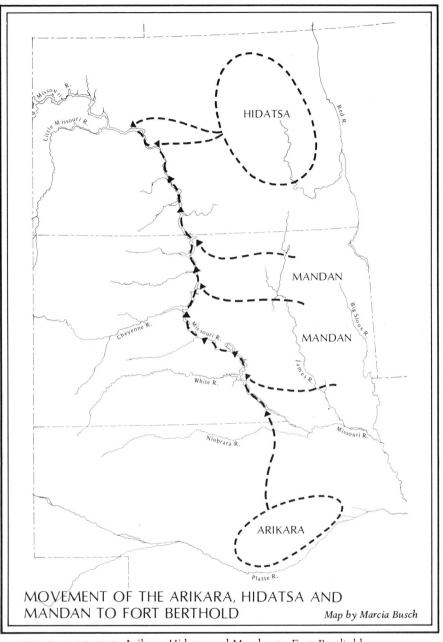

MOVEMENT OF THE ARIKARA, HIDATSA AND
MANDAN TO FORT BERTHOLD

Map by Marcia Busch

MOVEMENT OF THE Arikara, Hidatsa and Mandan to Fort Berthold.

tion publicized it as a potentially rich source of trade. By the time Lewis and Clark had returned in 1806, entrepreneurs were planning to launch trading parties up the Missouri, using St. Louis as a major base of operations. Indeed, the beginnings of this type of enterprise had already occurred during the Spanish ownership of Louisiana in the late 1790's. Now, however, new companies entered the picture — the Missouri Fur Company, the Rocky Mountain Fur Company, and the colossus of the trade, John Jacob Astor's American Fur Company. Manuel Lisa was among the first to establish himself solidly on the Upper Missouri, having been one of the organizers of the American Fur Company, which operated from the mouth of the Platte to the beginnings of the Missouri in Montana.

In 1807, Lisa established a fort at the junction of the Yellowstone and Bighorn Rivers, slightly to the west of what is now the Fort Berthold Reservation. Still, his company faced many problems. The Blackfeet Indians, among others, grew hostile and helped to break down the trading venture. Worse yet, the fur traders themselves — crude, rough, and boisterous — fomented unpleasant incidents that soon turned the Arikara, who were then located in what is now northern South Dakota, into the archenemies of the American traders. The Rees soon acquired a reputation as the most treacherous of the Missouri River tribes. In all fairness, however, their unsavory reputation was primarily a product of their adamant refusal to allow themselves to be intimidated by the somewhat arrogant traders.

Other great names in the fur trade also appeared on the Upper Missouri during this period. Pierre Choteau of the Missouri Fur Company led parties up the river to contact the Mandans, the Arikara and the Hidatsa. Choteau was in the process of establishing both a fortune and a family, one which is prominent in St. Louis to this day. The War of 1812 forced the Americans to abandon much of the Upper Missouri region, while the British continued to work the area. Nonetheless, Manuel Lisa remained and continued to promote the interests of the United States. Lisa proved to be instrumental in keeping the three tribes fundamentally neutral during this war, but after the conflict his company declined steadily. Lisa himself died in 1820, and the Missouri Fur Company very soon suffered a similar fate.

In 1822, the Rocky Mountain Fur Company was organized by General William H. Ashley to trade on the Upper Missouri. The original expedition went upriver during that year, as did an expedition from the American Fur Company. In 1823, Ashley himself led a group to the region with the firm intention of stopping at the Arikara villages near the mouth of the Grand River, in what is now South Dakota. There he planned to trade for horses, but was instead attacked and defeated. His men then retreated down the river, tacitly admitting that the Arikara had succeeded in closing the great route into the interior of the continent. This was the height of Arikara power; they would never again be so strong.

Ashley appealed to the Army, which in response sent Colonel Henry Leavenworth from Council Bluffs to punish the Arikara. In this campaign, Leavenworth's 220 troops were reinforced by men from the Missouri Fur Company and by Ashley and Henry, along with four or five hundred Sioux warriors. Even though they struck at the Arikara villages with a combined force of between 800 and 1100 men, they were repulsed in the immediate fighting. The Army had performed very badly, and the Sioux regarded them as cowards. The Arikara, although they abandoned their villages by night, took understandable pride in their accomplishment. They were more determined than ever to prevent the penetration of the region from the south.

The Arikara opposition to the fur trade was stimulated by several factors. They had traditionally been the middlemen in the Indian trade in the Upper Missouri country. Long before any white traders had entered the area, they had traded their agricultural products and their highly prized decorated robes for meat and raw materials from other tribes. When the horse trade first appeared in the area, the Arikara again assumed the role of middlemen, but made the enormous error of trading the first horses to the Sioux. They had, in effect, forged the weapon that nearly destroyed them later. In the 1820's, however, they were at full strength and determined to remain so.

A second expedition, under General Henry Atkinson and Major Benjamin O'Fallon, next came north in 1825 and concluded a treaty not only with the Arikara, but also with the Mandans and the Hidatsa. By this time, Astor's pride and joy, the American Fur Company, had established its western department and had merged with several of its competitors. It threw up posts on the Upper Missouri and assigned the famed "King of the Upper Missouri," Kenneth MacKenzie, to that region. MacKenzie's men had put in operation a post to exploit the Mandan trade at the time the Arikaras moved up the river to settle near the Mandans. The Arikara pressure forced MacKenzie to abandon his post for a time.

During the 1820's, rivalry in the fur trade increased substantially, as the Columbia Fur Company, the American Fur Company, and Hudson Bay Company all competed in the same region. By 1830, however, the American Fur Company had again reestablished its superiority, which it would retain as long as the fur trade remained a viable business. The retirement of Astor himself in 1834 brought a dissolution of his company, but its old subdivisions continued to function under different ownership, and the trade itself went on, although its profits continued to decline as the years passed.

The effects of the trade on the Indians of the region grew out of the methods and the tactics that were used. Fur traders locked in economic combat with each other and resorted to practically any means to gain an advantage. For example, they meted out large quantities of liquor to the Indians, which had a sustained demoralizing effect on the tribesmen who were unused to it. Indeed, at one time, MacKenzie actually established a distillery on the Upper Missouri, quite contrary to the laws of the United States, which forbade the use of spirits in the Indian trade. Liquor was important, and at times was a decisive expedient, but it was not the only enticement used in the trade. Beads, pots, kettles, mirrors, guns, and textiles were all an important part of the business. Many of these things were highly desirable to the Indian people. Indian women, who had long been skinning buffalo with stone knives, saw immediate advantages in instruments made of steel, and they had no desire to return to the use of home manufactures once they had been introduced to such new delights. Thus, today's luxury became tomorrow's necessity. Not only were the techniques of home manufacture and other cultural attributes lost, but also self-sufficiency and independence were now casualties. These people, who had formerly shifted entirely for themselves, now became dependent on outside resources. They would also now begin to bicker and fight with other Indians for possession of areas containing fur-bearing animals. Moreover, the Indian male, who in the past had always been a man performing many functions, now became a specialized hunter and trapper. The goods themselves stimulated the rise of many new desires among the Indians, and led to the unflattering traits that so often accompany overwhelming greed. None of this boded well for the Mandan, Arikara, and Hidatsa peoples. Their isolation, which had served as their greatest protection in the past, had come to an end. They were now being forced to coalesce in order to withstand the pressures of a white society, whose advance agents were trading with them, and to guard against the relentless Sioux, who continued to advance on them in great numbers, all the while gaining in wealth and power. The fur trade had brought some technological advantages to the Indian and a slightly higher standard of living, but the price they paid was indeed exorbitant by any standard.

RELATIONS WITH THE
U. S. GOVERNMENT

The three tribes had contact with white traders out of Canada in the eighteenth century and had gained some familiarity with Americans early in the nineteenth century, particularly because of the Lewis and Clark expedition. They went for many decades, however, before achieving a degree of formal relations with the United States government common to most Indian peoples. This was primarily due to the isolated nature of the area in which they lived and to the inability of the new republic to properly administer the Louisiana Territory and its myriad Indian peoples. In 1819, the United States established the Upper Missouri Indian Agency with its headquarters in St. Louis. The agent in charge very seldom visited the outer reaches of the region under his care, however, and the three tribes — together with other groups like the Assiniboine and the Crow — were pretty much ignored. Indeed, it was not until 1851, through the Treaty of Fort Laramie, also called the Horse Creek Treaty, that the boundaries of the land of the three tribes were established and anything approaching a reservation came into being. Under the provisions of the Horse Creek Treaty, the government confirmed the claims of the Mandan, Arikara, and Hidatsa people from the right bank of the Missouri to the mouth of the Heart to the mouth of the Yellowstone, with the area enclosed by those streams and a vague line drawn from the mouth of the Powder River to the headwaters of the Heart. According to the treaty, the three tribes were not compelled to relinguish their claim to any other land or to their accustomed hunting grounds. At this time, the Mandans and Hidatsa were living, for the most part, in a single village at Fort Berthold while the Arikara were still lodged near the mouth of the Knife River. It was not until 1866 that all of the three tribes had coalesced at Fort Berthold.

In 1864, Washington divided the Upper Missouri Agency and appointed an agent who was given specific responsibility for the three tribes, together with the Assiniboine and the Crow. After 1870, the three tribes finally had their own agent.

Relations with the United States government were, if anything, more crucial to the three tribes than to most Plains Indians. Surrounded as they were by enemies on every side, ruined by epidemic disease, and feeling a severe loss of strength, the three tribes needed much help, and the American government — as will be seen — was slow and inadequate in giving it.

THE PLAGUE YEAR OF 1837

Few people have had to withstand anything as awful as the smallpox plague of 1837, which ravaged the Three Affiliated Tribes and other

Indian peoples. The Indian people had no natural immunity to this disease and no effective way of treating it. The white men knew about vaccination, but were unable to innoculate even the majority of their own people, let alone the Indians who were scrattered over the Upper Missouri country. Thus, the Indians had no resistance to the disease, and the result was incalculable horror.

The plague struck in July. It has long been asserted that smallpox was transferred to the Indians from the steamboat *St. Peter,* whose crew unloaded cargo on the Upper Missouri in that month. On the other hand, some recent research indicates that this may not necessarily be so. It is certain, however, that the origin of the epidemic lay with the white man, for the disease was unknown in North America before Caucasians began exploring and settling the continent.

When the plague came, it spread with devastating speed and violence. The victims experienced pains in the head and back and then died within a few hours. Their bodies turned black and swelled to perhaps three times their normal size. Almost everyone who caught smallpox died; hundreds died every day. With so many deaths, burial proved impossible, and the corpses were thrown over cliffs.

The Mandans were the first to be hit, while the Arikara and Hidatsa contracted it later. To the Mandans, it seemed that the white man was to blame for their plight and that whites were somehow protecting the latter two tribes, while allowing them to be destroyed. As a result, an angry Mandan brave attempted to kill the fur trader, Francis Chardon, but failed. Even the beloved chief, Four Bears, a long-time friend of the white man, turned hostile and in a dramatic speech urged his people to "rise all together and not leave one of them alive." Yet, the disease was so ferocious and so all-consuming that it not only overwhelmed the Mandans physically but also psychologically. Although individuals might strike out in retaliation, as a group, the people were completely demoralized and totally incapable of launching any kind of a concerted attack on the whites.

The terrible dread of this disease also led to suicides among the Indian people. Near Billings, Montana, is a cliff where Crow warriors leaped off in sheer desperation. A young Mandan shot his own wife, killing her to prevent any further suffering. One young warrior even dug his own grave and lay down in it, and there died.

The epidemic raged through the summer and into the fall. The Hidatsa and Arikara escaped the worst of it by scattering along the Upper Missouri. The Mandans, however, remained in their village largely because Sioux war parties prevented them from moving, and thus they were nearly decimated.

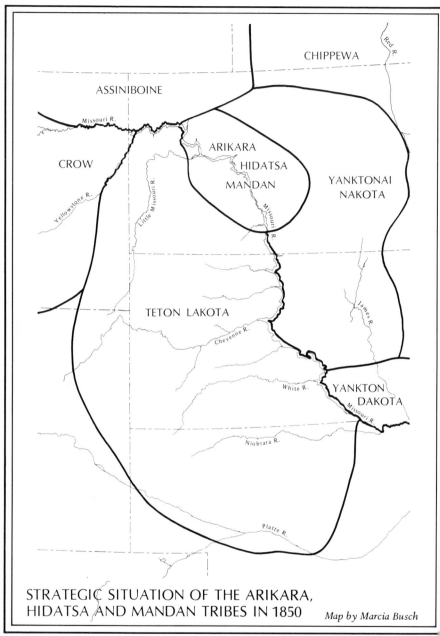

STRATEGIC SITUATION OF THE ARIKARA, HIDATSA AND MANDAN TRIBES IN 1850

Map by Marcia Busch

STRATEGIC SITUATION OF THE ARIKARA, Hidatsa and Mandan Tribes in 1850.

George Catlin, the great artist of the west, explained their plight graphically:

> The Mandans were surrounded by several war parties of their more powerful enemies the Sioux, at that unlucky time, and they could not therefore disperse upon the Plains, by which many of them could have been saved: and they were necessarily enclosed within the piquets of their village, where the disease in a few days became so malignant that death ensued in a few hours after its attacks: and so slight were their hopes when they were attacked, that nearly half of them destroyed themselves with their knives, with their guns, and by dashing their brains out by leaping head foremost from a 30-foot ledge of rocks in front of their village. . .Nobody thought of burying the dead, whose bodies, whose families together, were left in horrid and loathsome piles in their own wigwams, with a few buffalo robes, etc., thrown over them, there to decay, and be devoured by their own dogs.

This was truly a disaster. While the population of the Arikara and Hidatsa were nearly halved, it has been estimated that the Mandan population fell from 1800 people in June to less than 100 by the end of the year. There are few examples in history of any people being so devastated by a disease in such a short period of time.

The Mandan Indians were in truth nearly extinct, and they knew it. They abandoned their villages on the Knife River, and the few that were left migrated farther up the Missouri. Some Mandans moved in with the Arikara, some with the Hidatsa and their old tribal organizations fell apart, as there were simply not enough people to maintain them.

By the summer of 1839, the Mandans had left the Arikara, with whom they had disputes, and joined the Hidatsa. The Hidatsa, in turn, fled the Knife River country to escape the disease and crossed over to the east side of the Missouri. There they made their way north, little by little, and in 1844 selected a site for their winter camp at a bend in the Missouri. The village they established was known as "Like-a-fish-hook" village. This settlement became the permanent home of the Hidatsa and Mandans, and the beginnings of Fort Berthold.

The American Fur Company sent Chardon to this village, where he hired Indian women to cut and drag the timber for the fort, which was originally known as Fort James, possibly named for one James Kipp. By 1846, the fort was being called Fort Berthold in honor of Bartholomew Berthold, the brother-in-law of the famed St. Louis fur trader, Pierre Choteau, Jr. The fort's future as a center of the fur trade was not sanguine. The fur trade itself was in a state of decline, and the Indian people in the area were weak in numbers and demoralized in spirit; as if that were not enough, they were also under

44

heavy pressure from their ultimate enemies, the Sioux.

SURVIVAL AGAINST THE SIOUX

The 1860's brought an increase in the pressure of the Sioux against Fort Berthold and its three tribes. For decades, these people had been pushed, shoved, abused, and mutilated by Sioux attacks. The impetus for the Arikara movement to the north had been Sioux hostility. In fact, the Sioux had been greatly responsible for forcing an uneasy coalition on these three peoples, who ordinarily would have preferred to live separately.

By 1860, the Sioux in their various divisions were reaching the apex of the most considerable Indian power ever seen on the Northern Plains. Directly in the path of this great warrior people huddled the remnants of the Mandans, Hidatsa, and Arikara. They were protected by an American government whose general inactivity and occasional corruption made it somewhat less than an adequate shield for its friends.

Under normal conditions, which seldom existed on the Plains, the three tribes would have been reluctant to ally themselves with the United States government. Now, however, they had little choice, for there was no other ally available. The advance of the Yanktonai in the north, the Teton divisions of the Junkpapa, Sans

Arc, Two Kettles, Blackfeet, and Miniconjou from the southeast, left them no recourse in that area. The Blackfeet and Assiniboine to the north and east were of no help to the three tribes, and their only possible Indian ally — the Crow — were under such intense pressure themselves that they could be of little aid. Therein lies the explanation for the close alliance with the United States of America, which no doubt saved the gallant three tribes, but at times must have made them wonder if it was worth it.

The United States, as has been pointed out, had all but ignored the Upper Missouri, although they had guaranteed land ownership to the Mandans, Arikara, and Hidatsa. This situation was adequate, as long as the peoples could defend themselves. In 1861, however, the Civil War broke out, and its effects were felt throughout the entire Northern Plains. It is probable that the British in Canada, who were at that time seriously considering entering the war on the side of the Confederacy, were encouraging Indians to trade in Canada and to move against American posts. The Sioux, in particular, increased their raids, and turmoil continued on the Plains. At the same time, as the Union government concentrated its war efforts east of the Mississippi, regular troops were moved out of the Plains region and were replaced by volunteer units that too often lacked both military skill and organizational ability. For a time, Con-

THE HIDATSA-MANDAN NUETA COMMUNITY – Crow's Hearts Place. This dramatic view of a tipi settlement highlights one military weakness of the Mandan, Hidatsa and Arikara when they moved frequently in summer to avoid Sioux attacks or to hunt on the Plains. Cooking fires at dusk turned every tipi into a beacon guiding Sioux scouts to Three Affiliated Tribes camps. The Arikara, Hidatsa and Mandan moved within a circumscribed area, so enemy Sioux did not need to search far to locate settlements to raid, by their evening lights or other give-away signals.

federate prisoners — the so-called "Galvanized Yankees" — were stationed at Berthold to protect the post from the Sioux. These men were given the choice of either serving in a prison camp or in a Yankee garrison in Indian country. They were not, to say the least, the most dedicated soldiers available. At the same time, the problem of supplying the Upper Missouri became increasingly critical. In peacetime conditions, transportation to this area had always been difficult, and supplies often arrived late and sometimes not at all. Under wartime conditions, the situation was even worse, as the government concentrated its major efforts elsewhere. Necessary Indian supplies, if they were available at all, came late and were administered by second-rate men, as more talented individuals were inexorably drawn to the major theatres of the Civil War. Thus, a combination of factors put the people of Fort Berthold in a desperate situation, and one over which they had very little control.

Yet another factor should be mentioned among the mounting problems of the Three Affiliated Tribes. The gold strikes that occurred in western Montana at this time meant that an increasing number of white men would be passing through the region, and that a major government effort would be made to supply the prospectors in the gold areas, mainly because the Union needed the precious metal to help finance the war effort. The Missouri River supply route never received the publicity that the Bozeman Trail through Wyoming and Montana did, and it never resulted in gaudy confrontations like Red Cloud's War. It did, however, by funneling steamboats and wagons to the region, increase the restlessness of the Sioux, and thus also increased the danger to the tribesmen around Fort Berthold.

It might be asked why these people, who had successfully lived on the Plains for centuries, were in such a defenseless position. For one thing, they were essentially a sedentary agricultural people who lived in fixed habitations. Under such circumstances, they lacked mobility and the ability to duck and dodge, to feint and foray. Their population was down considerably because of the smallpox attacks, and their opposition was mounted, superbly fitted to hit-and-run cavalry warfare, and vastly superior in numbers. Thus, the Mandans, Arikara, and Hidatsa can best be described as the stationary targets, while the Sioux were the aggressive attackers that could strike from any direction at any time with superior forces. This was indeed the period of greatest danger for the three tribes and a time when their very existence hung in the balance.

One of the immediate effects of the Sioux penetration of the area around Fort Berthold came in the winter of 1861-62, when the

Arikara were forced to vacate their previous dwellings and move into a temporary settlement above Fort Berthold. In March of 1862, they crossed the river from the fort and began to construct a permanent village. Within a short time, however, they were attacked by the Sioux, and by August they had moved back across the river and re-joined the Mandans and Hidatsa. This was the final and permanent union of the three tribes, and from this point on, they operated in relation to outside forces and pressures as a unit. The Sioux, by their unceasing hostilities, had forced this action upon them.

It is true that while the United States government neglected their Indian friends on the Upper Missouri, some people expressed concern. William Jayne, the Governor of Dakota Territory and Superintendent of Indian Affairs, wrote Washington that more help was desperately needed for "the only tribe belonging to this agency who have been and remain sincerely friendly to the government." He blamed part of the problems of the united tribes on the fact that their friendship with the American government had increased the hostility of the Sioux.

The Sioux continued to raid constantly, driving off horses, plundering stores and killing the great Hidatsa chief, Four Bears, when he was only a mile from his village. For this treachery, agent Samuel N. Latta demanded reparations

50

from the Sioux, who were getting payments and equipment from the government, while the friendly Mandans and Hidatsa were receiving very little. To him it appeared that the policy of the government was calculated to bribe unfriendly Indians and to ignore those who supported the United States. Latta further requested military protection for the three tribes and increased appropriations for schools, instruction, housing, mills, and other needs, but to no avail.

The arrogance and audacity of the Sioux continued. On Christmas Eve of 1862, a war party estimated at 600 Sioux attacked Fort Berthold. Their strategy was to fire the houses in the Indian village so that the smoke would cover their attack on the fort itself. Not only did this fail, but the Indians in the fort attacked the Sioux and beat them soundly. Nonetheless, most of the fort and a greater part of the Indian village had been destroyed in this encounter. As a result, the three tribes moved into a nearby and newer fort, originally named Fort Atkinson, which had been built as an opposition fur post. It now served as their major bastion of defense against the seemingly irrepressible Sioux.

The Sioux defeat in 1862 only seemed to increase the frequency and the ferocity of their marauding. On one occasion, a mackinaw boat carrying gold from Montana was sacked and its crew killed by the Sioux. In 1863, a new factor was introduced into the already troubled situation. The eastern, or Santee, Sioux had engaged in a war in Minnesota in 1862, where they were defeated and driven out after severe difficulty. The Santees, homeless and wandering, became a malignant catalyst among their western relatives and did much to disrupt conditions on the Upper Missouri. As a result, the United States government finally decided to begin extensive military operations on the Northern Plains. General Henry H. Sibley led an expedition from Minnesota into Dakota, while General Alfred H. Sully brought another force up the Missouri River and overland to Devil's Lake, where they expected to trap the Santees between the two columns. As usual, however, the government was unable to distinguish between friendly and unfriendly Sioux, and the plan misfired. Sibley's column did little good, and the Minnesota Indians remained in Dakota Territory, unhappy, angry, and looking for trouble. Sully, on the other hand, although he had failed to meet with Sibley, surprised a party of Sioux at White Stone Hill in September of 1863, and fought a spirited battle, in which the Indian casualties were very high. Sully then returned south, and the fruits of the victory disappeared as the sullen Sioux continued to roam freely on the Upper Missouri.

During this time, Santee Sioux approached the Mandans, Arikara, and Hidatsa, and tried to interest them in an alliance against the white man. The negotiating parties met only three miles from Fort Berthold, where the allied tribes refused the offer. A small battle ensued among the Indians, and other problems soon followed. The situation at Fort Berthold was becoming very critical — indeed, almost hopeless. A steamboat carrying the necessities of life to the three tribes was attacked by the Sioux in the vicinity of the fort, and it never arrived. The Mandans, Arikara, and Hidatsa were by now nearly starving; they were unable to hunt, their agriculture suffered, and the Sioux drove off their horses, all it would seem because they remained friends with the whites.

Famed missionary Father DeSmet attempted to arrange a peace treaty with the Sioux but failed. In 1864, White Shield, premier chief of the Arikara, addressed the United States and said:

We are afraid of the Dakotas: they will kill us, our squaws and children, and steal our horses. We must stay in our villages for fear of them. Our Great Father has promised us soldiers to help keep the Dakotas out of our country. No help has come yet. We must wait. Has our Great Father forgotten his children?...We want our Father to bring us guns to hunt with, and we want dresses, coats, pants, shirts, and hats for our soldiers, and a different dress for our chiefs; we want a school for our children. Our hearts are good. We do not speak with two tongues. We like to see our white brothers come among us very much. We hear bad talk, but have no ears. When we hear good talk we have ears.

In 1864, Father DeSmet actually got some of the Sioux to agree to a peace treaty, but General Sully refused to accept it and was determined to chastise the Sioux. As a result, he led still another expedition into Sioux country and routed several thousand Sioux in the battle of Kill Deer Mountain, using cannon. When Sully arrived at Fort Berthold, he detached a company to garrison the post, and for the first time, the United States Army was in a position to defend its friends. This military occupation continued until 1867 when the troops were removed to a point seventeen miles farther east, where they established a post called New Fort Berthold. The old fort had never been owned by the government. Later, the new post was dubbed Fort Stevenson and was built to quarter 238 men. In the years following, the conditions among the tribes at Fort Berthold continued in the same pitiful state. The Indians, still living in almost total poverty, nonetheless refused to give up their loyalty to the United States. To add to their difficulties, the administration of the reservation at this time was rife with corruption. In practice, this meant that the little the tribes should have received was reduced further in the wake of the illegalities committed by their agents and traders. Moreover, during this same time, the tribes were also forced to face one of the periodic cycles of drought and crop failure, combined with yet another smallpox epidemic. Things were truly bad.

In 1869, crop failures continued, as did the unending enmity of the Sioux. In June of that year, 500 Sioux warriors rushed the Fort Berthold village, touching off a brief battle. The Sioux were driven off, but while the three tribes suffered only half the casualties of their opponents, they could afford them much less than the Sioux, and worse, the whittling down process continued. On January 2, 1870, 200 Sioux warriors struck again and this time were driven off with cannon fire by troops from Fort Stevenson.

As the 1870's began, the Indian wars started to die out in that area of the Dakota Territory, and in 1871 the last of the fur trading companies, Durfee and Peck, sold old Fort Berthold to the government as housing for the Indian agency. A more stable period was in the offing. Yet the Mandans, Hidatsa, and Arikara, although receiving some respite from Sioux attacks, were in a sordid state and were finding it difficult to maintain life. They found, to their dismay, that hostile Indians who gave trouble to the government still continued to receive more food and gifts than did those who were the friends of the white man. Even this did not weaken their loyalty. During the campaigns of George Armstrong Custer, including the one that led to his classic defeat at the Little Bighorn, Arikara scouts, led by the famous Bloody Knife, were at his side, always reliable and always fighting for the United States against the Sioux.

One may argue that the Mandans, Arikara, and Hidatsa chose the wrong side in the Indian wars of the 1860's and 1870's, and that they were truly let down by their allies. Yet, in reality they had no real choice. There was never any really viable opportunity to join the Sioux, and the United States' help — tardy, corrupt, and inadequate — was better than nothing. The notion of the united Indian movement, wherein all the tribes would fend off the white man, had very little meaning on the Upper Missouri in the 1860's and 1870's. The three tribes took the only course open to them, and they survived. The quality of their life was greatly diminished, their power was reduced to practically nothing, and indeed, they were barely able to hold on. By the end of the 1870's, however, their ancient enemies, the Sioux, were placed on reservations in South Dakota, and a chance to build a new life was now open to the gallant remnants of these determined people.

DESTRUCTION OF THE LAND BASE

Over the years, the Mandan, Arikara, and Hidatsa people had suffered great losses from disease, war, and starvation. Their land provided no exception to this pattern. Land losses began at the time their land claims were recognized in 1851 and have continued until the present day. By executive orders and congressional acts, their reservation, which started out with approximately 12,500,000 acres, was steadily reduced in size, until just before the Garrison Dam was built in the 1940's, it consisted of only some 643,368 acres. Even this latter figure is deceptive, because part of the acreage was owned by individual white men.

The first of the major reductions was introduced by executive order on April 12, 1870, according to which the southeastern boundary of the reservation was defined as a line from a point on the Missouri four miles below Fort Berthold to the junction of the Little Powder and the Powder Rivers. This amputated an area north and west of the Heart River that had previously been included in the 1851 treaty. The same executive order, however, did acknowledge a claim to a tract north of the Missouri.

The next attempt to shrink their land base came in 1880. The Northern Pacific Railroad had received a land grant from Congress to construct a transcontinental line from Minnesota to the Pacific. The grant specified that all the land south of a line forty miles north of the right-of-way was to be restored to the public domain, together with a large area south of Fort Buford Military Reservation. This represented a vast diminution in the amount of territory owned by the three tribes, and in order to compensate the Indians, their holdings north of the Missouri were extended to within thirty-five miles of the Canadian border and west to the White Earth River. It should be noted that executive orders are not negotiated, nor need they be ratified. The Indians were not consulted in either case, and as a result, these people, who had been long-time friends of the whites and of the United States, became increasingly bitter. Their loyalty seemingly was to be repaid by land losses.

On December 14, 1886, an agreement was negotiated with the three tribes, and it was about time. By this arrangement, they received lands north of the 48th parallel, which consisted of the area north of the present New Town, North Dakota, and lands west of the north-south line drawn six miles west of the most westerly point of the Big Bend in the Missouri. This agreement was not ratified by Congress until 1891, and under it the Indians were to receive $80,000 in annuities — that is, annual payment — for a period of ten years. One small addition to the reservation was made in the 1890's. It was discovered that, under the 1886 agreement, the 12th meridian had been set as the eastern boundary of the reservation, and that this stipulation would have placed the agency and some of the Indian farms outside the reserva-

Courtesy Paul A. Ewald

AMPLE "DANCES, CEREMONIES, AND TOM-FOOLERY" in the view of devout Christians that they tried to extirpate with federal power. Above: Arikara Black-tail Deer Dance. Below: Four Rings on an Arikara altar inside an earth lodge.

tion. Thereupon, the necessary boundary change was made on June 17, 1892.

The final alteration in the external boundaries of the reservation came in 1910. At this time, Congress, which no longer dealt in treaties or agreements, passed an act that authorized the tribe to sell everything north of township 150, plus four townships south of that line. This piece of legislation resulted in reservation boundaries that were retained until the 1940's, when the Garrison Dam project on the Missouri River took the better part of the bottom land available to the Mandans, Arikara, and Hidatsa. The dam was part of the Great Missouri River Dam System, and flooded approximately 155,000 acres of the best land on the reservation. This reduction represented a loss of more than 25 per cent of the total area of a reservation which, at the time, only had about 700,000 acres anyway.

THE "RESERVATION PERIOD"

Although the three tribes had survived both smallpox and the Sioux, their future was still in doubt. They had been an agrarian people during most of their recorded existence, but on the upper reaches of the Missouri, agriculture is difficult and crop failures are common. They continued to farm and hunted when able, although these economic pursuits became more and more unfeasible. They began instead to rely upon the subsistence provided by the agencies of the United States government, and this in turn tended to create a state of dependency, which militated against the preservation of their culture and institutions.

There can be little doubt that the United States government fully intended to destroy the native lifestyle of the American Indian, in order to make him a functioning part of what modern politicians have called the "mainstream" of American society. During the 1870's and 1880's, the agents at Fort Berthold, even though they might have been sincere in their wish to help the Indians, worked continually to alter the Indian lifestyle. One of these agents, William Courtenay, suggested that the government should forcibly put an end to the Indians' "tribal organization, dances, ceremonies, and tom-foolery." He further asserted that the Indians should be compelled to work, and if they balked, they should be allowed to starve. Courtenay's proposal was never fully implemented, but the government's policy certainly pointed in the same direction. The only difference was that it was carried out in a desultory fashion and at a slower pace.

One of the means the government used to break down Indian culture and to make imitation white men of the native peoples was education. On the Fort Berthold Reservation, a school was opened in 1870, soon closed, and

61

then opened again in 1873, after which date it continued. In 1876, Reverend Charles L. Hall began missionary work calculated not only to educate, but also to Christianize the Indians. In 1884, the government set up a boarding school in the buildings at Fort Stevenson, which had been abandoned by the War Department. Then in 1889, Father Francis Craft began working for the Catholics on the reservation and soon established a Catholic boarding school there. The government tried to ensure attendance at all of these schools by denying rations to any Indian family whose children did not enroll. Strict discipline was enforced in all of the schools in question. The children's long hair was cut off; the boys were put in military uniforms; and the girls were attired in the prim dresses suitable for Victorian maidens. Demerits of one sort of another, complete with appropriate punishments, were meted out to any child who dared to revert to the use of his native language or native customs.

In a sense, the educational system involved a kind of forcible and intense brainwashing effort. One of the great tributes to the strength of the Mandan, Arikara, and Hidatsa cultures was that these educational exercises basically failed to achieve their purpose. It is true that the Indian students did learn to speak, read and write English, and did master the appropriate manual and domestic skills. Yet the old ways were not

Courtesy Paul A. Ewald

HE SUMMER SEASON TECHNOLOGY of the Three Affiliated Tribes for centuries ncluded "bull-boats" made of buffalo-hide stretched over wooden frames, paddled ack and forth across the wide Missouri River.

destroyed in the learning process. The tenacity of all American Indians for retaining their way of life and a sense of values precious to them is truly astounding. The whole force of the government and of American religion and education was unable to abrogate their life style.

Another attempt made to turn the Indians into "typical" Americans, however, began when the government moved to encourage and enforce the individual ownership of real estate, and to scatter the people, who had always lived in villages and farmed the surrounding area communally. The goal was to make them into American type farmers, each on his own plot of land, and each separated from his neighbor by a good substantial fence. For the majority of American Indians, this process, called severalty, did not start until the passage of the Dawes Act in 1887. The Mandans, Arikara, and Hidatsa, however, were chosen, possibly because they had been such worthy friends of the United States, to be the recipients of severalty prior to the passage of the Dawes Act, which in the end would nearly destroy what remnants of the continent remained to the American Indian.

As early as 1882, twenty Indian families from the three tribes left their village to farm on the other side of the Missouri as individuals. Three years later, the entire population joined in this process. One cannot be entirely certain about the effectiveness of the government pressure to

Courtesy Paul A. Ewald

GARDENERS MAY SHELL BEANS BY HAND, but farmers thresh them by other means. This Hidatsa farmer is threshing beans in the traditional manner. Hidatsa, Mandan and Arikara farmers stored threshed, dried beans in large quantities to help subsist their families during the long, cold winters.

place the people on individual plots of land. Certainly, some of the tribal members wanted to take advantage of severalty; but it is likely that many others did not. Regardless, the process and the pressure ground on. In 1885, the agent told the tribesmen that unless they moved onto individual allotments, all government assistance to them would be withheld. Under the weight of such threats, most of the tribe decided to give it a try. By sheer good fortune, the harvest that year was bountiful. In their country, where wheat is a major crop, the results of planting are always either good or bad. Because in this case they were good, by 1886 nearly everybody moved onto allotments, and the old village was abandoned. During the same year, a treaty was negotiated whereby the reservation would be surveyed so that the process of allotment could proceed. Because there was more land than there were individual Indians at that time, there was a land surplus; and the three tribes ceded all right and title to their land north of the 48th parallel. Thus, the size of the reservation was greatly diminished, and the people were dispersed on their own individual farms. Even this, however, failed to destroy their culture.

By 1895, the government regarded the allotment process for the three tribes as substantially complete. Nine hundred forty-nine of the allotments were along the Missouri River, the area best suited for agriculture. In 1910, another 765

Photograph by Monroe Killy

CROW FLIES HIGH'S SON DRAGS WOLF in 1942 when nearly eighty years old. Drags Wolf became chief of the Shell Creek Community on the reservation. He persuaded the Bureau of Indian Affairs to establish a day school there so children would not have to leave home for an education. When representative government came in 1936, Shell Creek elected Drags Wolf to the first tribal council. He served until 1941, and died on August 24, 1943.

allotments were established, some on the river, others in the foothills. One thousand one hundred thirty-one allotments were made in the upland areas between 1912 and 1915, and finally, 556 more were made between 1923 and 1929. Part of the allotment system provided that after a certain period of time, a "competent" Indian could receive a patent in fee to his land and with it United States citizenship. As was usual on most reservations, when the Indians received the patent, they frequently sold the land to white men, thus further reducing the land base of the reservation. One further aspect of the system dictated that those who did not sell their land or did not receive a patent in fee would have their plots divided among their heirs. As the years went by, the numbers of people holding undivided interests in a particular piece of land became very large indeed. The problems of trying to work under these conditions were mind boggling, and remain mind boggling to most scholars who have studied them. Much of the land could only be used by leasing it, again to white men, and in some cases could not be used at all.

Leasing, of course, was not a complete disaster for the Indian people. It did give them an income which might not have existed under the normal conditions of land ownership. Anyone who leases land for someone else to work can, however, seldom receive the full benefits available from that land. There is, of course, nothing dishonest in this, and if one cannot profitably work his own land, it may be the only way to make money. Certainly it requires less effort on the part of the landholder. Yet at the same time, the leasing process has caused ill feeling, as many Indians have grown to resent the idea of white men making a profit off their land.

Another of the results of allotment involved the exodus of a small number of the people from Fort Berthold. This grew out of an incident, in which Crow Flies High coveted a chieftainship. The other chiefs refused him the position, and as a result, he and a band of Hidatsa and Mandans, numbering about 185, left the reservation and moved to Fort Buford. They remained there until 1884, when they were ordered away by the post commandant. They then settled on the Little Knife River, west of Fort Berthold, and lived by hunting and fishing. In 1886, the followers of Crow Flies High requested that they be taken back onto the Fort Berthold Reservation. The United States government was amenable to this, if the people agreed to take individual allotments, build houses on their farms, send their children to school, and in general act like the government expected a "good Indian" to act. The seceders refused the offer and remained outside the reservation for some years.

69

Here was an adamant rejection of the government policy of individual ownership, and also a dramatic presentation of a basic rift in the peoples of Fort Berthold. This fissure centers on what is frequently referred to among Indian people as the "half-breed/full-blood split." The terms are not really correct. The split is rather between those who feel that it is desirable to accept the white man's way of life as quickly as possible, and those who reject this course in its entirety. Most Indian people fall somewhere between the two extremes, but incline toward one side or the other. In an area where three tribes are forced to live with one another and to reconcile tribal differences, this philosophic difference adds considerably to the tensions and makes the compromises that are necessary for life and progress to continue much more difficult. It is a tribute to the good sense of the Mandans, Arikara, and Hidatsa that they have been able to overcome this.

Under allotment, the logical result would ordinarily be for the people to cease to live together in communities and instead live individually on their own farms. The urge to live communally proved to be very strong, however, and when Like-a-Fish-Hook village was abandoned in the 1880's, new communities were established. Like-a-Fish-Hook village had never really been a full fledged and natural community, because the people had clustered there primarily as a measure of self-defense against the Sioux. When they left it, they established more comfortable villages, and the United States government unknowingly aided them by establishing day schools in these communities. Thus, the government – and not for the first time – outsmarted itself by institutionalizing the very associations that they wished to avoid. Such places as Lucky Mound, Elbowoods, Independence, Armstrong, and Shell Creek were founded in this period and allowed the people to live according to their tribal commitments to a greater extent than had been possible previously.

The Bureau of Indian Affairs, which administered Fort Berthold in the twentieth century, became more and more paternalistic and turned increasingly to education as a major means of enhancing the acculturation process. The Indian agents were replaced with school superintendents, and the office of agent at Fort Berthold was abolished officially in 1904. At the same time, there was a steady increase of tribal members leaving the reservation to obtain their education. Such famed Indian schools as Haskell and Carlisle trained many of the future leaders at Fort Berthold.

Most of the Plains Indians suffered terribly in the agricultural depression of the 1920's. Fort Berthold and the affiliated tribes, however, found a cushion to help ease their plight. In 1920, Congress authorized the Court of Claims

71

to hear the tribes' case concerning the land taken without compensation under the executive orders of 1870 and 1880. In 1930, $2,169,168.50 was awarded to the Three Affiliated Tribes as compensation for the loss of their land. The court arrived at a figure of 9,846,186.93 acres for which the Indians were to be paid 50¢ an acre. After deducting "gratuities" of over $2,750,000, the final figure was determined. The members of the tribe received the money on a per capita basis, and the distribution of the funds was supervised by the agency. The tribe made a few other attempts to gain compensation for white injustices committed during the nineteenth century, but very little availed.

During the 1920's, with excellent prospects for obtaining revenue from the government, the people at Fort Berthold made definite progress, particularly in wheat farming. By the late 1920's and early 1930's, however, they had been pretty much wiped out by a combination of low prices and severe drought. By 1934, the Three Affiliated Tribes, who had had their ups and downs, were in a definite state of decline, and people were living in harsh poverty. It was clear that the policies of individual land ownership, education, and Christianization had failed, and that the Indians, like other Americans, had not escaped the devastation of the Great Depression. When Franklin D. Roosevelt assumed the presidency in

1933 and started his New Deal, it was apparent that a new deal for the Indians was in order, and indeed such a program had already begun as early as 1929 in the administration of Herbert Hoover. In 1934, the Indian Reorganization Act passed, and the Mandans, Arikara, and Hidatsa would once again start working their way upward toward prosperity.

THE INDIAN REORGANIZATION ACT, DEPRESSION, AND WORLD WAR II

Until the Indian Reorganization Act was passed in 1934, the Fort Berthold people had been operating under forms of government that were both weak and lacking in legal sanction. This act, stemming from the Merriam report of 1928, provided for many improvements, including increased medical, educational and economic aid for the Indians. Its most lasting effect, however, came from provisions that allowed tribes to organize themselves, establish constitutions, and become self-governing. The Bureau of Indian Affairs, led by Commissioner John Collier, went to great lengths to see that as many tribes as possible accepted this act and created governments under its provisions. At Fort Berthold, meetings were held on various parts of the reservation, and the proponents and their antagonists engaged in serious and sustained debate. There were a number of reasons why so many people supported it. The educated

Indians, who saw distinct advantages in any system that would give them the opportunity for self-expression, were, of course, behind this act. The young businessmen, ranchers, and the like also generally could see advantages in the law; and even some of the traditionalists, highly conservative in their outlook, embraced it. The interests of the traditionalists were different but valid. Many of them felt that the act gave the younger generation a chance to assume governmental responsibilities like those which their ancestors had enjoyed. Still others appreciated the religious freedom granted by the act. Under its terms, old ceremonies could be resumed, and the Native American Church could be introduced on the reservation. On the other hand, some conservatives opposed the act as something now offered to them by the white man and thus something to be mistrusted. Others pointed out that little could be achieved through the tribal government without the approval of the Secretary of the Interior, and if everything done had to be approved by a cabinet officer, it was really not self-government. When the verbal battles were over and the election held, the act passed narrowly, and a constitution and by-laws were adopted and approved on June 29, 1936. The tribal government was immediately organized after the appropriate elections were held.

One other aspect of the IRA presented the possibility of chartering the tribe as a corpora-

Photographs by Slough, Courtesy Monroe Killy Collection

CONDITIONS ON FORT BERTHOLD RESERVATION in the summer of 1942. The rounded earth-lodge had changed into a European-style vertically-walled structure. The children illustrate graphically how rapidly the Three Affiliated Tribes population recovered from its 19th century low point after peace reached the Northern Plains.

tion under the Department of Interior. This gave the tribe the potential for borrowing, investing, and in general, acting like a corporate body in business affairs. Under the IRA, this also had to be put to the people in a separate election, and again, the old debates broke out. The charter passed, however, and was approved by the Secretary of the Interior on April 24, 1937. Thus, the Three Affiliated Tribes, whose basic friendship and trust of the Americans had been historic, continued in this tradition and moved toward new forms of tribal government. It has been argued that elective government is not appropriate for Indian people, because leadership has been traditionally established by consensus on a semi-hereditary basis. It should be pointed out, however, that the old leadership had not functioned effectively since the late nineteenth century, and thus the new governmental arrangements were not replacing older forms, but rather filling a vacuum. The people, most of whom had never voted in any election, moved slowly to participate in the government. In the period leading up to World War II, the tribal government made much progress toward organizing and establishing itself. Very little in the way of dramatic legislation occurred because there was little about which to legislate. During all this time, on the other hand, the people were learning about the way democracy worked: how

Photographs by Slough, Courtesy Monroe Killy Collection

CEREMONY CONDUCTED AT ELBOWOODS, North Dakota, on the Fort Berthold
eservation, for a returned Marine Corps veteran in June of 1942.

to vote, how to campaign, how to serve on councils, and how to serve as tribal presidents. The political foundation they built in the 1930's would prove very useful when they fought the battles surrounding the Garrison Dam issue in the 1940's and 1950's. The political base was indeed solid, and the tribal government grew progressively stronger in succeeding years, until it can now be regarded as one of the more successful on the Northern Plains.

Much of the help the Indians received in the 1930's came by way of the New Deal programs designed to relieve the economy. The Works Progress Administration, Public Works Administration, Emergency Relief, dam-building, conservation, the Civilian Conservation Corps, and all the rest did much to alleviate the suffering of the individual Indian. Indeed, it can be argued that the late 1930's represent one of the more prosperous periods for the majority of Mandans, Arikara, and Hidatsa. Yet, this phase was transitory. When World War II broke out, the New Deal relief programs were dismantled on the grounds that prosperity had returned. On the Fort Berthold reservation, prosperity had not returned, and there was probably more suffering and poverty in 1943 than there was in 1938. Yet, the Indian people responded nobly to the war effort, as they had always done in previous wars. The young men went to war and fought well. The people at home survived, but many of them had to leave the reservation and take jobs connected with the war effort in other locations. Some remained off the reservation permanently, but more returned when the war ended.

The end of the war brought with it the return of the servicemen to the reservation, who were a new class of people. The boys, who had left the reservation, returned as men who had traveled the globe, who had led others in crucial situations, and who had learned the skills and techniques of leadership. They now moved into tribal politics very quickly, and furnished the leadership that would take charge in the crucial times ahead. It is no exaggeration to say that the United States Armed Forces were the staff college of tribal leadership for several decades following the end of the Second World War.

THE GARRISON DAM

When the Congress of the United States passed the Flood Control Act of 1944, Public Law 534, it set in motion events that were to have the most grave effects upon the Three Affiliated Tribes. Its immediate result was to spawn two plans for controlling the Missouri River above Sioux City, Iowa, and then unite them into the Pick-Sloan plan. As finally conceived and constructed, it called for the building of a series of enormous earthen dams in the

79

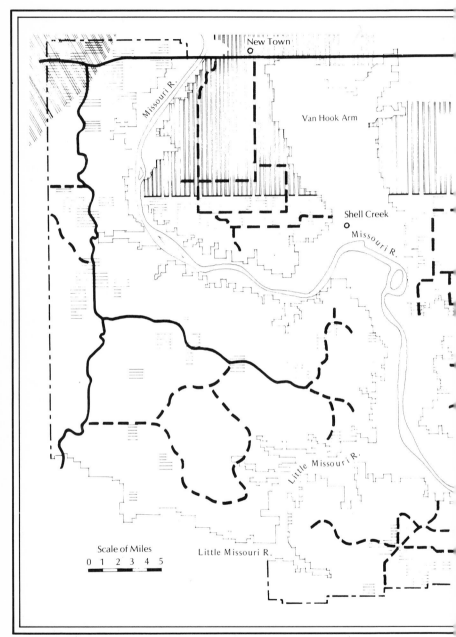

FORT BERTHOLD RESERVATION TODAY.

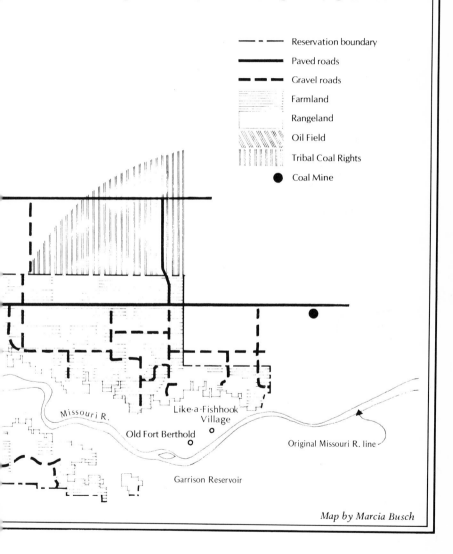

Reservation boundary
Paved roads
Gravel roads
Farmland
Rangeland
Oil Field
Tribal Coal Rights
Coal Mine

Missouri R.

Like-a-Fishhook Village

Old Fort Berthold

Original Missouri R. line

Garrison Reservoir

Map by Marcia Busch

Dakotas that would effectively tame the Great Muddy at the cost of flooding most of the bottomlands in two States. Support for the program was broad and effective. The Dakotas, Montana, and Wyoming wanted the potential irrigation. Iowa, Nebraska, Kansas, and Missouri wanted flood control. All wanted electrical power. The Mandan, Arikara, and Hidatsa wanted the whole thing dropped as one of its key elements was The Garrison Dam which would be built near the southern border of their reservation. They organized and fought in Congress and in the courts. They fought well and hard, but they lost in the face of over-whelming opposition. In the losing, they paid as high a price as any people can pay for "progress."

Any tribe that had survived the smallpox epidemics and had shaken off the onslaught of the Sioux could have been reasonably expected to do nicely in the peace and quiet that pervaded the middle of the twentieth century. Yet, the building of the Garrison Dam and the subsequent filling of its reservoir disturbed their lives as much as any of their previous disasters. As has been mentioned, the reservoir behind the dam flooded over 25 percent of the reservation. The lands it inundated were the bottom lands, containing the richest and most productive soil on the reservation; but the dam's adverse effects extended well beyond this. In the end, it also buried much of the cultural structure of the tribe, which had been built so painfully over the years.

Prior to the filling of the Garrison reservoir, 90 percent of the reservation population lived on the Missouri Valley bottom lands. As a result, 90 percent of the people were torn from their homes and relocated on the highlands. Forced relocation is always traumatic, even for an individual or a family. When it is done to 90 percent of a people, the effects are awesome. All organizational forms and structures were drastically altered; friendships were ripped apart; community cohesion was totally dissolved; and the habits and customs of generations were almost completely destroyed. All of these elements now had to be rebuilt practically from scratch.

The awful physical effects themselves should not be ignored either. Seven day schools were located on the reservation; all of them were lost. Elbowoods, the agency headquarters and the home of the boarding school, was moved. Every child who had been attending school on the reservation was forced into a different educational environment when it was all done. The whole pattern of physical rebuilding seemed to undermine any aura of permanency.

Moreover, 80 percent of the road system of the reservation had been located in the area flooded by the dam. As a result, when the people were relocated, they were put into areas

83

where there were virtually no roads. A system of 230 miles of new highways had to be built. Even so, communication facilities were inadequate, because the huge lake behind the dam had cut the reservation into five districts, which were not readily accessible to each other. Thus, the people of the reservation became more and more divided, and it must be assumed, frustrated.

The people on the reservation had developed a fairly natural economy by the end of World War II. There were springs and creeks that provided water, exposed coal beds offering a fuel supply, and plenty of timber on the river bottoms for fuel, building materials, fenceposts, and winter cover for livestock. The valley contained the wild fruits and berries that supplemented their diet. The dam wrecked the entire system. Coal mines were flooded, as was the timber, the fruit, the berries, and very nearly the people themselves. A whole new life had to be established in the midst of considerable bitterness. More and more, the people were forced from a natural economy to a cash economy, without the wherewithall to sustain themselves.

It is true that the Mandans, Arikara, and Hidatsa were paid for the land that they lost; but a lump payment failed to compensate for a lost lifestyle. For the most part, the money was paid to individual land owners, and, for the most part, portions of it were spent unwisely and not used for capital investment. Thus, the people

Photograph by Joseph H. Cash

FOUR BEARS LODGE, the magnificant motel complex on the shore of Lake Sakakawea, owned by the Three Affiliated Tribes.

were worse off than they had been before. Prior to the building of the dam, the great majority of people were self-supporting. With the dam, and even with the large payments, came a dependency on welfare and the social problems that usually accompany such a lifestyle. The environment itself changed; and the people, who had always lived close to nature, now had a different kind of nature to deal with.

The many advantages that can usually be expected to flow from the construction of a major dam in dry water country have not as yet materialized for the Three Affiliated Tribes. They are having great difficulty in retaining the legal rights to the water that are and should be available to them. They see their great potential resource going to serve the white men in areas other than their own. They see plenty of electric power, but their people are unable to make the optimum use of it. The industries that could be spawned by the presence of power, water and labor have not come in any numbers, and those that have developed have not as yet proven terribly successful. They are attempting to exploit the recreational possibilities of the area and have built a magnificent motel complex, the Four Bears Lodge, to provide proper accommodations. The area is still quite isolated, however, and it may be decades before the tourists, who can sustain such an operation, come in sufficient numbers to make the situation profitable. All in all, the dam has been the third major disaster to strike these people. Unlike the other two, it has a built-in potential for good. Unless the government and the people themselves move rapidly to take advantage of this potential, however, it will not be realized, and the unhappiness and dislocation will continue.

THE FUTURE

The Mandan, Arikara, and Hidatsa people are looking to a future that is full of promise, one that will lead them to a better and more prosperous life than they have had in the past. With 5200 members enrolled in the Three Affiliated Tribes and with 2000 of these living on the reservation proper, they do not face insoluble population pressures. Their hopes for material well-being are based on solid factors and not simply desire. Morale is high among their leadership, and the people themselves are becoming more and more involved in their own decision making. All of this points to plans realized and not expectations denied.

One of the great dreams of the Affiliated Tribes is to repurchase more of their land base. The first step in making this dream a reality lies in preventing land held in individual allotments from going into the fee simple title status, because that would allow the land to be sold out of Indian hands. The tribe has set aside $1,500,000 to purchase land and is one of the first tribes in the nation to launch a major land

Painting by Karl Bodmer, Courtesy University of South Dakota Library

ARIKARA SCALP DANCE or battle victory celebration.

buying operation. As good businessmen and strong agrarians, they are buying land in the eastern sections of the reservation, 90 percent of which is for farming. Still, approximately $300,000 of tribal funds is being used to purchase grazing lands in the western districts. The land itself, once purchased, will provide income for buying yet more land or for other tribal programs, if the tribe should choose to do so.

A tribal asset, which has not been fully exploited, but which remains and becomes potentially more valuable as the crisis in energy increases, is its coal reserves. There is, for example, a vein of coal on the reservation that ranges from four to seventeen feet in depth and contains an estimated 17 billion tons of low-grade lignite that has not been touched. It may well be that the time has not yet arrived for the maximum use of this resource. In any case, the tribe is in no hurry to work the deposits and feels that the value of its coal can only increase as time passes.

Yet another windfall is the presence of oil on the reservation. There are not the quantities of oil that can be found in many other areas of America, and most of the reservation oil wells are privately owned and thus of no direct benefit to the tribe. The possibility of further exploration and development exists, however, and, with increased demand, such efforts could well provide higher yields and greater income for the members of the tribe. The tribe is also vitally interested in developing an extensive system of irrigated farming, which would utilize the waters of the Garrison reservoir. Under these circumstances, the Garrison Dam, which inundated so much of the reservation's resources, might yet prove to be a marked advantage to the tribe, if the federal government and the state can be persuaded to allot the proper water rights and to capitalize the necessary irrigation programs. This is, of course, a long-range proposition and may take years to develop. Yet the demand for wheat and other farm products is rising and food shortages are becoming more and more obvious throughout the world. Because of this, the tribe believes that in the long run it has an excellent chance of implementing a successful irrigation program and by so doing would not only increase its income, but allow more of its tribal members to work the land themselves. At the present time, a great many of the tribal land owners lease their property, because they lack the capital and technological know-how to properly maintain and operate it. Irrigated farms are smaller and more easily financed, however, and thus under such an arrangement the Indian could cease to be an absentee landlord and become instead a more independent, and hopefully more prosperous, farmer.

While the tribe is not pleased with the record of industry on the reservation, it still expresses some hope that in the future industry may develop into a major area of employment for tribal members. The presence of coal, oil, water and electrical power, together with a considerable potential labor supply, should eventually attact to the reservation some solid and stable industries. At present, in New Town, North Dakota, Northrop Dakota, Inc., which makes airplane parts, employs 80 people, nearly half of whom are tribal members. It is a going concern, and, as a subsidiary of a major corporation, Northrop seems likely to remain and conceivably could even expand. Other such factories might eventually come to the reservation, but distance is a major factor working against such a development. Fort Berthold is far from any major market, and transportation costs tend to eat up profit margins on any high bulk and high weight items that have to be sent a long way. On the other hand, light weight, easily shipped products, such as electronic components and the like, represent a practical possibility on the Berthold Reservation and lead one to believe that the future lies there. Thus, the tribal government remains convinced that in a matter of thirty or forty years, the reservation can become economically self-sufficient and that federal subsidies and welfare programs will no longer be needed. Their estimate seems reasonable in light of their present situation.

One of the major areas that concerns the tribe and the local citizens is education. While the white man's education may have been a device for breaking down Indian culture in the past, it is now regarded as a necessity for both the present and the future. People at Berthold proudly state that the Three Affiliated Tribes have a higher percentage of their young people in colleges than any other reservation in the country. At the same time, they are also concerned about their local school systems. Their sons and daughters go to schools that are, for the most part, fully integrated and of adequate quality. Yet, in none of the schools is there a coordinated program aimed at teaching the culture and languages of the Indian people. Tribal members are working to develop courses of study and methods of teaching the three languages in the school systems and anticipate that within five years this program will be fully operative. Certainly one cannot argue effectively that the life, history, culture, and languages of our original inhabitants are not a suitable subject for study in an American school system. Moreover, such a program of Indian studies may be able to retain much of value, which might otherwise be lost to posterity, and at the same time it might also help to develop more mutual understanding and respect between the Indians and the white man. This is the thrust of and rationale behind the Indian educational program, and there seems to be some basis for assuming it will succeed.

All that has been and will be accomplished on the Fort Berthold Reservation will inevitably funnel through tribal government, which must provide the necessary leadership if the projected improvements are going to reach fruition. That tribal government seems to be highly operative and very functional. In the last five years it has become increasingly subtle and skilled in its ability to conceive, plan and direct highly complex programs, in addition to its role in conducting the day-by-day business that any government must handle. Part of this growth in effectiveness is undoubtedly due to pressures from below. The people have become more active in tribal decision making, as illustrated by their extensive use of the referendum, and by their growing general participation in the politics of their tribe. Tribal politics by their very nature are unstructured and lack institutions. Political parties do not matter in tribal elections, nor have tribal political parties sprung up in any organized sense. Thus, a great deal depends upon the personality and charisma of each individual candidate, and the only real check on him is the close regard that his constituency pays to his actions. Yet this tribal government has functioned well. It failed to stop the construction of the Garrison Dam but has succeeded in making the best of the bad situation dealt to its people. The tribal government was active in the establishment of the United Tribes of North Dakota where it worked in concert with representatives of the other tribes in the state. This was most unusual, because the dominant people in the state are the Sioux, the ancient enemies of the three tribes. Now they work together around the same council table.

One of the most far-reaching events in recent Indian history was initiated by the Three Affiliated Tribes. This was a court case dealing with the question of who had jurisdiction of the areas ceded in the aftermath of the allotment acts. The tribe contended that when the land was ceded, the reservation boundaries still remained the same and that therefore it had jurisdiction over them. The county governments in the state of North Dakota, on the other hand, claimed that the reservation boundaries had been wiped out with the land cession and that jurisdiction and all its aspects rested in the state and its political subdivisions. The decision sustained the view of the Three Affiliated Tribes, that is, that they did indeed have jurisdiction. When the dam forced them to move their headquarters to New Town, which was really a white community totally controlled by white people, they faced a

94

situation that was, in all due frankness, pretty much anti-Indian. The tribe, under the court decision, acquired jurisdiction over New Town and yet had the foresight and forbearance not to assert its power completely. In truth, all the tribal leaders demanded and received was control over law and order matters to help guarantee a fair shake for their people. By so doing, they avoided trouble with the white residents of the area, and yet still managed to protect the major right they were interested in. The other rights coming out of this decision still remain, but the tribe has wisely chosen not to press them. The so-called New Town decision actually consists of two decisions rendered in 1971 and 1972, which are now forming the basis for similar actions by tribes all over the Northern Plains. Thus, the Three Affiliated Tribes led the way, as indeed they may lead the way in other matters.

Above and beyond the factors related to economics, education, and government, are matters of the spirit that cannot be measured nor entirely described. The Mandans, the Arikara, and the Hidatsa are proud people on the move and on the rise. They are retaining and sustaining their culture and their lifestyle. Their heritage is important to them, and they are determined to preserve it. At the same time, they are intent on making their way in a modern world that moves faster than anyone can anticipate. They have suffered, they have died, they have been nearly exterminated. Yet, their genius for survival and for revival has brought them through critical situations and will again. They have their problems, yet problems are common to all great Americans. These Tribesmen can and will overcome them and achieve a future more shining and more worthwhile than anything they have lost in the past.

SUGGESTED READING

Very few historians have attempted to write a general history of the Mandan, Hidatsa, and Arikara peoples. Of necessity, therefore, many of the works cited below deal with rather specific aspects of the life and development of these three tribes. The authors believe that this collection will prove very useful to the reader who wishes to pursue the subject further. It must be emphasized, however, that this list is by no means exhaustive, and that many other scholarly books and articles about the Three Affiliated Tribes have been published, and should be available to the reader in most major libraries.

BOWERS, ALFRED W. *Hidatsa Social and Ceremonial Organization.* Washington: U.S. Government Printing Office, 1965. Smithsonian Institution Bureau of American Ethnology. Bulletin 194.

This is the most complete treatment of the Hidatsa social and ceremonial organization.

BOWERS, ALFRED W. *Mandan Social and Ceremonial Organization.* Chicago: The University of Chicago Press, 1950.

This is the most thorough description and analysis of the Mandan social and ceremonial organization.

CHARDON, FRANCIS. *Chardon's Journal at Fort Clark, 1834-1839.* Annie Abel (ed.). Pierre: Published under the Auspices of Lawrence K. Fox, Superintendent, Department of History, State of South Dakota, 1932.

This is a primary source of some interest, with an excellent historical introduction.

CURTIS, EDWARD S. *The North American Indian.* Volumes IV and V of twenty volumes. Cambridge, Massachusetts: Cambridge University Press, 1909.

This is a classic work, which provides an excellent description of the three tribes as separate entities during their early years.

DE LAND, CHARLES. "The Aborigines of South Dakota," *South Dakota Historical Collections,* Volume III, Part 1. Sioux Falls: Press of Mark D. Scott, 1908, 271-584.

This effort is not well written but still contains useful information about various aspects of the history of the Arikara in South Dakota.

DE LAND, CHARLES. "The Aborigines of South Dakota," *South Dakota Historical Collections,* Volume IV, Part 2. Sioux Falls: Press of Mark D. Scott, 1908, 275-727.

Again, this work is poorly written, and yet is useful in describing the Mandan stay in South Dakota.

DENIG, EDWIN THOMPSON. *Five Indian Tribes of the Upper Missouri.* John C. Ewers (ed.). Norman: University of Oklahoma Press, 1961.

This is a primary source written by a famous fur trader dealing with the period of the early eighteen hundreds. Chapter Two is devoted to the Arikara and is extremely hostile in its tone.

DUNN, ADRIAN. "A History of Old Fort Berthold," *North Dakota History,* XXX (October 1963), 4-88.

This is a splendid secondary source for the period through 1900.

ROBINSON, ELWYN B. *History of North Dakota.* Lincoln: University of Nebraska Press, 1966.

The standard one volume history of North Dakota. Robinson is superb in placing the three tribes in their historical setting.

SCHULENBERG, RAYMOND. "Indians of North Dakota," *North Dakota History,* XXIII (July-October 1956), 4-116.

This work is perhaps the best general source extant dealing with the cultures and lifestyles of the three tribes from the eighteenth century to the nineteen fifties.

SPICER, EDWARD H. (ed.). *Perspectives in American Indian Culture Change.* Chicago: University of Chicago Press, 1961.

Chapter Four, written by Edward Bruner, provides an excellent synthesis of the development of the Mandan culture, including material on the more recent period.

TABEAU, PIERRE. *Tabeau's Narrative of Loisels' Expedition to the Upper Missouri.* Annie Abel (ed.). Norman: University of Oklahoma Press, 1939.

An interesting and excellent primary source, this effort, dealing with the late eighteenth and early nineteenth centuries, contains a very useful historical introduction.

WILSON, GILBERT L. *The Hidatsa Earthlodge.* Bella Weitzner (ed.). New York: The American Museum of Natural History, 1934. Anthropological Papers of the American Museum of Natural History, XXXIII, Part V.

This presents definitive data concerning the famous Hidatsa dwelling.

WOOD, W. RAYMOND. *An Interpretation of Mandan Culture History.* Number 39 in the Inter-Agency Archeological Salvage Program, River Basin Surveys Papers. Robert L. Stephenson (ed.). Smithsonian Institution Bureau of Ethnology. Bulletin 198. Washington: U.S. Government Printing Office, 1967.

This study provides a good account of Mandan archaeological discoveries and of Mandan pre-history.

JOSEPH H. CASH is Duke Research Professor of History at the University of South Dakota, Director of the American Indian Research Project and the South Dakota Oral History Project. He taught at Eastern Montana College before coming to the University of South Dakota. A native of South Dakota, Professor Cash earned his B.A. and M.A. degrees from the University of South Dakota, and the Ph.D. from the University of Iowa. He has conducted and directed oral history among a great many of the Northern Plains tribes, and has published on both Indian history and mining history.

GERALD W. WOLFF is Associate Professor of History at the University of South Dakota. He taught at California State University at Long Beach prior to assuming his present position. A native of Ohio, Professor Wolff has the B.S. and M.A. degrees from Bowling Green University, and the Ph.D. from the University of Iowa. A specialist in Nineteenth Century American History, he has published numbers of articles in professional journals. Professor Wolff has interviewed American Indians about their history for the American Indian Reserach Project at the University of South Dakota, and is presently working on several manuscripts.

PHOTOGRAPHS

The rich pictorial record of Mandan, Hidatsa and Arikara life during the past 150 years sampled in this volume deserves a word. The authors arranged with the University of South Dakota Library to make color photographs of the London edition of Bodmer's paintings, which was colored by the artist himself.

Photographs of the World War II conditions at Fort Berthold come from the collection of Monroe Killy of Minneapolis, Minnesota. He spent many years in the field of photography, and is a charter member of Indian Tribal Series.

Other historic photographs come from the large collection of Paul A. Ewald of New Town, North Dakota.

104